Mrs. FreD Schrock

W9-CFP-534

Object Lessons
using common things

How to Teach Bible Truths
with Everyday Items

by J. E. DEGOLIA

SCRIPTURE PRESS PUBLICATIONS, INC.
WHEATON, ILLINOIS 60187

© 1954, world rights reserved
Scripture Press Foundation

Fourteenth printing, 1974

ISBN 0-88207-026-6

Printed in the United States of America

Contents

	PAGE
Our Flag and Our Bible	5
An Awl Blinds and Opens Eyes	9
Salt-of-the-Earth Christians	12
Kites and Prayer	16
The World's Greatest Food Factory	19
God's Word, A Plumb Line	22
Without Spot or Wrinkle	26
Seeds of Blessing	29
Coal, Moth Balls, and Perfume	33
Melody in the Heart	38
Spiritual "Shoes" That Fit	43
Lifeless Dolls or the Living Saviour?	47
Needful Nails	50
Wormy-Apple Christians	53
The Strongest Rope in the World	56
Obeying God's Safety Laws	60
Light-of-the-World Christians	64
Processed and Powerful	68
Cracked-Corn or Popcorn Christians?	72
Christian "Space Men"	75

You Can Make Common Things Work

As we study in the four Gospels of the New Testament the methods of the Lord Jesus, the Master-Teacher, we find that He drove home heavenly truths most frequently through the use of parables (Mark 4:33, 34). And what are parables? Their classic definition is "earthly stories with heavenly meanings" — in other words, Jesus explained unknown things of heaven by comparing them to well-known things on earth. If we would teach as the Master-Teacher taught, we too shall use object lessons, using familiar, easy-to-understand things of earth to make clear unfamiliar, hard-to-understand things of heaven.

These lessons are easy to prepare and are illustrated with objects that are readily obtainable. Because in some groups new children come and go, the plan of salvation is included in most of the lessons.

When presenting a lesson to the class, be so thoroughly familiar with the content that you are not at all dependent upon this book. You will do well to outline the message simply on a 3″ x 5″ card, to which you may refer if necessary. This will enable you to remember the important points. Practice the object lesson at home several times, preferably out loud, referring to the outline on your card as little as possible. Definitely depend on the Lord to prepare the hearts of each one in your class for the message that you will bring; and count on Him to drive home salient truths, so that the boys or girls may clearly understand how to know the Lord Jesus as Saviour and how to live so as to please Him.

Our Flag and Our Bible

THEME Respect for our flag and reverence for
our Bible.

MATERIALS A small flag of your country on
display; a Bible; pieces of red, white, and blue
cloth (or whatever colors are in your flag); sheets
of printed paper.

TODAY we are going to talk about our flag. What is a
flag? Someone says it's a piece of *cloth.* Is he right? Yes,
these pieces of colored cloth [hold them up] could be
cut and sewed together to make our flag. If we'd do that,
would we have only a piece of cloth? A flag is a piece of
cloth, but it is far more than that—it is the banner of
some country (the United States of America, the British
Empire, or whatever country you live in). Our flag is a
symbol of the righteous principles for which our country
stands, a guarantee of protection and security. Doesn't a
thrill of pride go up your spine when you see our beautiful
flag flying in the breeze?

When we see the *blue* of our flag, we are reminded of
the faith of early pioneers who trusted God even through
times of disappointment and danger. The *red* of the flag
reminds us of the sacrifices our forefathers made to es-
tablish this nation. *White* is always symbolic of purity of
heart and mind. (The symbolic meaning of colors varies
from country to country. Adapt this explanation to your
situation.) Yes, the colors of our flag stand for heroism,
truth, and righteousness.

Is there anything in these pieces of cloth by themselves [show them] to demand our respect? No, they
could be made into an apron as well as a flag. We could
even wash the floor with them or wipe our muddy shoes

on them. But we cannot use our flag that way! Because our flag represents the power and honor of our great country, it demands our respect.

Now, answer another question—what is a Bible? [Hold up Bible.] A book? The Word of God? Yes, both of those answers are right. As a book, the Bible is composed of sheets of paper that have been printed and bound together. These printed pages have been called the finest literature in the world. But if the Bible were merely sheets of printed paper [hold up sheets], even the very best of literature, we wouldn't reverence it and carefully obey its words. No, the Bible deserves our attention and our reverence because it is God's personal message to every man and woman, boy and girl. In this Book, God tells us how to receive His gift of eternal life and how to live to please Him. The Bible may be thought of as God's special banner that points the way to heaven for Christian marchers. And it is an inspiring banner that recalls courageous and sacrificial deeds performed by earlier marchers in the name of Christ.

One day a little Italian boy in our country was going home from school. He had not been here long, but he was anxious to become a good citizen. He saw a woman standing on a ladder, washing the windows of her house. Suddenly the little boy darted across the grass to the ladder and deliberately tipped it over so that the woman fell heavily to the ground. In almost no time police appeared and hustled the frightened boy off to the police station and later to the judge. In the courtroom the judge told the boy that good citizens don't act that way, and asked why he had done such a vicious thing.

The excited boy replied, "She maka da rag ofa da flag."

When the judge heard that, he checked and found that the injured woman had been using a flag—our flag—to wash windows! At that, the judge released the boy, and fined the woman for disorderly conduct.

Never must our flag be used as a rag, nor should it be

6

allowed even to touch the ground. Our country has definite rules regarding the use of our flag. When it is not on display, it must be carefully stored so that it will not be damaged. When it becomes shabby from wear, it must be burned, to avoid disrespectful treatment. Strict rules also direct the hanging of the flag in proper positions, and specify that its appearance must show that it has been carefully handled.

Does your Bible get careful handling, too? Or do you carelessly toss it anywhere? Perhaps your Bible has loose or torn pages that suggest rough handling and certainly make reading difficult. What kind of care do our Bibles, the inspired Word of our living God, deserve?

What do you do when our flag is honored in a public gathering? You stand at attention, don't you? And if you're a boy who's wearing a hat, you remove it and place it over your heart. Servicemen in uniform are quick to salute our flag.

How can we honor our Bible? We can show our reverence by listening carefully when the Bible is read— these are *God's words* to us! We can do even more than listen carefully; we can memorize and store up God's teachings in our hearts, where they will never be lost and where they'll guard against our enemy, sin (Ps. 119:11). In our thinking, the Bible should never be lowered to the level of other books, for the Bible was written by about 36 men who were under the special guidance, or inspiration, of God's Holy Spirit (II Pet. 1:21). These writers were kept from making a mistake, for God knew that millions of men and women and boys and girls must be able to depend on the Bible as giving the true way of salvation. Therefore we are attentive as this God-given Book is read.

(If your time is short, you may omit the following illustration and conclude with the last two short paragraphs.)

In World War II, American soldiers on Corregidor, the last American defense point in the Philippine Islands, were overcome by the enemy and forced into crowded, dirty prison camps. Their food was scarce, their strength gradually ebbed away, and their wounded comrades suffered terribly. Yet they kept hoping that the United States Army would march in to deliver them. But as days, weeks, and even years went by, their fading hopes almost died out.

The prisoners didn't know it, but American GI's were fighting their way toward the prison. A band of commandos had been assigned the mission of capturing that camp and freeing the prisoners.

One bleak evening the prisoners went to sleep as usual, but were awakened by strange sounds early the next morning. Shouts, weeping, and laughter of one of their companions filled the air. Finally the prisoners sighted the miracle that was so agitating their friend—the beloved American flag was flying from the camp flagpole!

No wonder the man was almost overcome with joy. That flag meant rescue, safety, justice, food, home, and loved ones. The brave commandos had silently overpowered the camp during the night and the helpless prisoners were delivered.

Boys and girls who have not yet asked Christ to be their Saviour are still prisoners in the chains of sin, and have no hope at all of freeing themselves. But if they will accept God's invitation, "Look unto me, and be ye saved" (Isa. 45:22), they will be rescued from the enemy. This is the very first step of obedience to God, and as the Holy Spirit helps a boy or girl to take this and further steps of obedience, he can claim all of God's great promises of security and blessing.

Thank God for our flag! Thank God for our Bible!

Are you a Christian? And are you proud of the Bible, and do you honor it, read it every day, and ask God to help you *live* its truths? Let's pray that we shall.

An Awl Blinds and Opens Eyes

THEME Persistence in prayer and work.

MATERIALS An awl or ice pick, an unfinished model airplane, embroidery work, painting, or any other articles that have been started and not finished.

BOYS, did you ever start to build a model airplane—and then quit? [Hold up an unfinished plane.] Girls, did you ever start to embroider a towel or paint a picture—and never finish it? [Display these.] My, how interested you were the first half hour, perhaps the first day or so! But something happened. The newness wore off, the glue didn't stick right, the thread knotted, or the paint didn't look right—so you got tired of the project and gave it up. Today it is just as unfinished as it was when you quit working on it.

These things remind us of certain Christians. After they have believed in Jesus as their Saviour from sin—and that is the only way one can become a Christian—they sort of give up and do not trust the Lord or exert themselves to develop their Christian character. That was what the Apostle Paul was rebuking the Galatians for. Paul wrote them, "Ye *did* run well; who did hinder you that ye should not obey the truth?" (Gal. 5:7). The Lord urges us through His Word to go on to perfection, or to the *completion* of the work that God has called us to do (Heb. 6:1). When we allow our interest to lag we look, in God's sight, like an incomplete person. Because the Lord doesn't want us to be quitters, He urges us to be *"steadfast, unmovable, always abounding* in the work of the Lord." He encourages us by reminding us that our labor "is not in vain in the Lord" (I Cor. 15: 58).

Has any one of you ever seen an awl, which looks somewhat like an ice pick? [Show whichever you have and comment on its sharp point.] Awls were used a great deal in days past in punching holes in leather while making harnesses for horses.

In the year 1812 a little boy in France had a horrible accident with an awl. As a result, he lost his sight completely. He was only three years old at the time.

Let's all close our eyes for a moment and try to imagine how we would feel if we'd never see the light again, never see another flower, bird, or the faces of our parents and friends. We'd feel sad because there wouldn't be much we could do to help others, and we'd know that others would often have to help us.

But Louis, the little boy who lost his eyesight, didn't spend time feeling sorry for himself. As he grew older, he determined that he would go on and finish the work that he thought God wanted him to do. He went to school with children who could see, for there were no special grade schools and high schools for the blind, as there are today. Yet he learned his lessons, became a fine organist, then went to Paris Institute for the Blind. At the age of 19, he became a teacher in that school.

One day, in a restaurant, a friend told him of an army captain who was sending most unusual messages at night to his men who were stationed where no light was permitted. The captain had been punching holes in pieces of paper and the men would read his messages by feeling the holes with their fingers. Suddenly Louis jumped to his feet and began to shout. Then, remembering where he was, he sat down saying, "Now I can open the windows so the blind can see!"

Louis started working with all the enthusiasm that anyone could have—as you did when you started making something (point to unfinished articles). But days, weeks, months went by. Working out a simple alphabet of holes was a slow job. Five years went by. Finally Louis appeared before the Institute for the Blind with a whole book printed with raised dots. He read part of it to the teachers. But instead of clapping for him and being grateful for his work, they claimed that he had memorized the portion he read. They rejected Louis' work—after five years of sacrifice, time, and effort!

But Louis didn't give up. He didn't stop, though he had reason to. Blind people came to his home secretly. With an awl [show this again]—the tool that had made him blind—he punched holes in paper—and taught these blind friends to read.

While Louis was dying, at the early age of 43, someone brought him word that his system had been accepted and that blind people would be able to read. Eagerly Louis exclaimed, "Thank God, my life has not been in vain!"

If Louis Braille had only *started,* and then had given up, he could never have had the joy of knowing that his life counted for something. Neither can you, if you get into the habit of quitting what you start.

Do any of you know what *persistent* means? It means *keeping on, enduring, continuing without change.* The Lord wants Christians to be persistent in prayer and work, not quitting if God chooses to withhold the answer for a time. Are you persistent in praying, or do you usually quit praying about something or somebody after a few days? If you will faithfully ask the Lord to give you the endurance to keep on praying, even when things seem hard, He will help you to finish jobs that you start, and He'll surprise you with wonderful answers to your prayers.

Salt-of-the-Earth Christians

THEME Living God's Word and witnessing for Him.

MATERIALS A small salt shaker, a medium-sized one, and a large one, all filled with salt; a pretty but empty shaker; a glass of water, a glass of salt water, and an egg.

(Because of the many uses for salt, this lesson has more comparisons than the rest. Read it carefully and choose only those that you feel will best clinch the aim you wish to stress.)

WHAT is salt? A little boy once said, "Salt is what makes potatoes taste bad when you leave it out." Without salt food certainly tastes flat. Salt is a combination of two chemicals, sodium and chlorine. When they are combined, they make this necessary chemical substance which helps our bodies to keep healthy.

Many interesting stories are told about salt. In Rome, years ago, servants were paid with salt, and from the Roman word "salarium" comes our word *salary*. American Indians called salt "magic white sand." Centuries ago a man could divorce his wife if she'd fail to salt his food. Many orientals, in the past as well as today, feel that salt used at a meal is a sign of friendship and hospitality. In fact, Arabs feel that if they have eaten salt together they are friends, and therefore cannot fight, for they say, "There is salt between us."

Do you remember that Jesus told Christians, "Ye are the salt of the earth"? (Matt. 5:13). Therefore, we can learn something about what a Christian should be by finding out some facts about salt.

Salt is taken both from the earth and from the sea. But no matter where it comes from, salt must be cleaned, or refined, before we can use it to season our food. How does this remind us of Christians? As salt is found in different places, so are we—we do not all come from the same kind of homes, and we are not all the same kind of sinners. But all of us need Christ as our Saviour and Cleanser. All of us were once without hope. "All we like sheep have gone astray; we have turned every one to his own way; and the Lord hath laid on him the iniquity of us all" (Isa. 53:6). "All have sinned and come short of the glory of God" (Rom. 3:23). That is why we need to be cleansed. We cannot serve the Lord until He cleanses us and refines us as we follow and obey His Word.

In early days men searched for important salt deposits, and often traveled to them. In this way, the first highways of trade were developed. As a result, communities, towns, and cities were built up, and progress was encouraged. Christians have furthered progress too, by obeying Jesus' command to carry the Gospel to the far ends of the world. Wherever the Gospel message is carried, not only are men's hearts changed, but their ways of living are changed, too. Those who believe God's Word become concerned with the needs of others. They work hard to better living conditions, and wherever the Gospel is carried, churches and schools and hospitals are built. Living conditions are improved. Women are treated with far more respect.

Men have found at least 14,000 uses for salt, in the various types of industry. But we use it chiefly as a seasoning for food—to bring out the flavor and make food taste good. Salt makes a difference in whatever it touches. Can you see why and how the Christian's testimony to the wonderful work of Christ is like seasoning food with salt? We read in Colossians 4:6, "Let your speech be always with grace, *seasoned with salt,* that ye may know how ye ought to answer every man." Suppose our speech isn't seasoned with salt. Suppose we fail to tell others of our love for Christ. If so, God says that we are like food with the salt left out.

We are not, of course, to put so much salt in food that we cannot taste anything but salt. Salt is supposed to call attention to the food, not to itself. Neither should we Christians over-salt our conversation by calling attention to ourselves. Our heavenly Father intends that we exalt our Saviour. Water with much salt in it is called *brine*. You and I are to show that Christians do not live a sad, hard, briny-salt life, but a happy, free, well-seasoned or balanced life. Joys are brighter, work is lighter, and life is fuller as we count on the Lord Jesus to "season" us properly. Our words and actions should prove to unsaved people all around us that there is a big and blessed difference in our lives, for we truly have far more than they. Then they will want to know Jesus as their Saviour, too.

Can you think of other uses for salt? It is used by leather and food processors to preserve hides and meat, by textile manufacturers, by road builders, by makers of soap and refrigerators, and by chemists for medicinal purposes, such as eye baths, mouth washes, and foot baths. Its use for preserving makes us wonder what Christians can do to help stop the spread of sin, the rottenness and disease of iniquity. We who love the Lord should be able to encourage those who are sick or discouraged. As salt in water makes objects float, so we who are Christians can bear burdens of others. (Illustrate by dropping an egg first into a glass of plain water, then into a glass of salt water.) Both of these glasses contain the same kind of water—but notice, there's salt in this second glass and it lifts the egg! Does this help you to see that if you're a "salt of the earth" Christian, your testimony that God is faithful will help to encourage someone else and make his burdens lighter?

Salt also puts out fire. James tells us in God's Word, "Our tongue is a fire" (James 3:6). So your testimony can stop the fire of gossip or lies. If salt is sprinkled in an oven where juice has run out of a pie, it will keep the spilled juice from smoking. Your salt-like behavior can prevent even sin-loving companions from "raising smoke"—doing wrong and evil things. Salt also breaks up ice in cold weather and makes slippery places safe so that people can walk without falling. Your testimony might be just what some weak relative or friend needs, to keep from falling into sin. The Lord wants each of us who love Him to be ready always to tell that He is real and ready to help (I Pet. 3:15).

What if salt loses its quality of saltiness? It is good- ← for-nothing! It cannot season food, preserve meat or hides, nor be of value in making soap or other chemical compounds. It would not be able to accomplish the thousands of things for which it is daily used. If you are a Christian who has lost your testimony for the Lord, you are useless to Him.

What can we learn from these different salt containers—this very small one, this medium-sized one, this large one, and this very pretty but empty one? [Hold up each shaker as you refer to it.]

Would you use this tiny salt shaker to salt potatoes when you put them on to cook? No, you would use this large one. But this little shaker is useful, too. It is an individual shaker, so handy to have beside your plate when Mother serves corn on the cob. Both of these salt shakers are useful because they are *filled* with salt.

Here is a pretty shaker [hold it up] but it is not filled. It is empty. Whether you are big or little, young or old, you are useless as a Christian unless you are filled with love for the Lord Jesus. Only if you're filled with His love can you be a blessing to those who need the Lord.

Surely our talk about salt has made us realize how important it is that we be true salt-of-the-earth Christians, and we shall be if we are constantly being filled with the Lord's own love and goodness. How can we be? By reading and obeying God's Word every day and talking to Him in prayer every day. Who would like to pray right now that we might become more and more the kind of salt-like Christians whom the Lord can use?

Kites and Prayer

THEME Believing prayer.

MATERIALS Several different kinds of finished kites; one unfinished kite; a piece of paper shaped like a kite, but without sticks, and decorated with pretty pictures.

THERE is nothing quite so thrilling in the spring as to fly a kite. But did you know that kites were not invented for boys and girls? According to the Chinese, kites were invented by their General Han Sin, 206 years before Christ was born, for use in war. Since then, kites have been used effectively by scientists and others.

You remember that Benjamin Franklin used a kite in his famous experiments with lightning and electricity. Kites have also been used by our weather bureaus. Men have attached thermometers to kites, to record the temperatures of clouds, thus helping to determine weather conditions. Kites have been useful in building bridges, in advertising, and to signal the movements of troops in war. They have been used in photographing enemy positions. During World War II they were standard equipment on life rafts, being used to attract attention and as aerials for sending radio messages.

Yet as we look at these kites [show them], don't you find it hard to believe that these flimsy kites can be so important?

Can you figure out any comparisons between kites and prayer? When you think of prayer, do you think only of the tiny children's prayer, "Now I lay me down to sleep . . ."? There doesn't seem to be anything particularly strong or powerful about reciting that prayer, does there? Who will read Matthew 21:22, what Jesus once said about true, believing prayer? Sue has read, "And all things, whatsoever ye shall ask in prayer, believing, ye shall receive." All things. That includes strength, courage, protection, power, and victory. It is tremendous what earnest prayer in the name of the Lord Jesus can accomplish in us and through us.

Though a kite is usually made of paper and sticks, any paper and sticks do not necessarily make a kite. Kites must be made with the right kind of paper and sticks and according to a plan, if they are to fly, and not be made just to look like a kite. This kite [show decorated one] was not made to fly. It was made to *look* like a kite—it's pretty, but it can't fly.

Though a prayer is usually formed of words, yet any words do not necessarily make a prayer. For our prayers to be lifted above this world, and to accomplish the things we desire to see done, we must follow the plan laid down in God's holy Word. Alice, will you read James 4:3? In this Scripture the Lord explains to us that sometimes we don't get answers to prayer because we "ask amiss"; that is, we want certain things for our own pleasure and enjoyment, rather than for God's glory. Such prayers, like the kites that some boys make, do not get off the ground.

Some kites look all right, but they aren't balanced right—or their sticks are too heavy—or their paper is not the right weight—they never will fly. Jean, will you read I John 3:22, and Mary, I John 5:14, to see how we can get answers to our prayers? These Scriptures make it clear to us that getting positive answers to prayer is not at all a matter of luck—it's a matter of believing and obeying God and asking that He give us what He knows is best.

The Chinese have a day each year on which everyone flies kites. Why? They do it to protect their homes, their families, and their loved ones from disaster. The story goes that a Chinese man, many, many years ago, dreamed that a terrible tragedy struck his home. His dream was so real that the next day he took all his family to the hills. There they flew kites all day. When they returned to their home in the evening, they found that it had been destroyed by fire. This man then believed that flying those kites had kept the demons away from his family. From then on, many Chinese have flown kites on the ninth day of the ninth month, to keep tragedy and trouble away from their homes.

All of you realize that a mere paper kite couldn't possibly scare any demons away. What a mistake, to trust in kites, instead of in the great Lord God, who has promised that He will be a refuge in the time of trouble, and will not leave those who seek Him in prayer (Ps. 9:9, 10).

Most of you want to pray often to your great Lord. But sometimes you get discouraged if God does not answer you right away. Jesus said, "Men ought always to pray and not to faint" (Luke 18:1). In other words, don't give up. Keep on praying—keep on believing God and He will answer your prayer in His best way at His best time.

Japanese boys think that if they fly kites made in the form of fishes over their houses, on a special boy's day, that they will become brave, full of courage and strength. But it takes more than a kite, made out of paper, sticks of wood, and string, to change anyone from a weakling, who is fearful and afraid, into a courage-filled person. This change can come about only through strong faith and confidence in the Lord (Ps. 138:3). He will help you as you pray to Him with all your heart. He invites you, "Call unto me, and I will answer thee," and He promises, "I will show thee great and mighty things" (Jer. 33:3).

The World's Greatest Food Factory

THEME A Christian's character and influence.

MATERIALS Elm, maple, apple or other leaves; an apple and an orange; word-card SUN-LIGHT.

WHAT do you think is the world's greatest food factory? No, it's not any cannery, cereal factory, soft-drink bottling company, or meat-packing establishment. Leaves are the greatest food factory! [Show leaves.]

This is hard to believe, but it's true. Leaves are the world's greatest food factory, for they actually take from the air and from the sunlight's radiant energy, some substances which we cannot see, and make food of them. This food is manufactured inside of every leaf that is in the light, silently and invisibly, day after day. Without this great food factory there would be no life on this earth. All people, animals, and plants would starve. You may have thought that leaves grow on trees just to make shade, or to make trees look pretty, but, you can see that they serve other purposes, too. The Lord put leaves on trees because they have definite work to do.

Leaves are not separate from the tree—they are joined to the tree. Running from the smallest root of the tree up to the topmost leaf on the highest branch, is a system of pipelines that carry water in and food out of every green leaf on the tree. Look closely at this leaf [show it], and you will see its veins. These veins are tiny pipelines that carry water in and out of each leaf. Through the leaf some of this water shoots into the air in an invisible spray, the leaf acting as a nozzle. A large elm tree may have several million leaves, and scientists tell us that it may release as much as a ton of water a day. An apple tree, which is smaller and has less leaves, may "spray out" as much as four gallons an hour. Can you understand now why it seems cooler under a grove of trees (or even under one large tree) in the heat of summer, than it does in the shade of a building? Trees are God's air conditioning plants.

Do Christians draw life and blessing directly from one source, as do leaves? Yes, all Christians are joined to the Lord Jesus Christ. He is our Source of supply, and even though most unbelievers may not know or realize it, Christians help to make the world a happier, safer, and more enjoyable place in which to live. But improving living conditions, and building hospitals and schools are not the first results of the Gospel. The Gospel's main message is that the Lord Jesus Christ, God's Son, died on the cross to make peace between the Holy God and sin-loving people. All who believe that Christ is their Peacemaker ("propitiation") are *saved* (I John 4:9, 10; Acts 16:31). The godly influence that Christians have on conditions and communities is somewhat like that of a tree whose leaves spray out cool, refreshing mist. One leaf wouldn't help much, but all the leaves working together make a shady area. Similarly, Christians may exert much more good by working together than they can all alone.

If you have ever visited any kind of factory you were shown both the raw material which came into the factory and the finished products that went out. Were you surprised at the great change that took place between these?

Since leaves make up the greatest food factory in the world, we are naturally interested in what raw material leaves use, and also what they make of it. [Display word SUNLIGHT.] Sunlight is one important raw material from which the leaf makes many products. A leaf is so constructed that it breathes from the underside, while the upper side has openings through which the sunlight enters and is trapped. From this energy the leaf develops food for itself—sugar and starches, and it feeds on this.

20

That food which the leaf does not need, it stores up for the tree's fruit. The apple tree's finished products are apples [show one]. The orange tree's products are oranges [show one]. Though water is brought up from the roots of trees, and the pipelines in the trunk and branches carry the extra sugar or starches to store in the fruit, it is the leaves that develop the actual fruit.

Did you know that God made trees grow in such a manner that every leaf gets the most benefit possible from the sun? The twigs and branches are so arranged that they do not get in another leaf's way. To really see how wonderfully God has made a tree, get under a large one and look up. You'll see how the leaves are arranged to face the sun. They turn on their stems to face the sun, which is their life, their strength. Did you ever notice that a house plant turns all its leaves toward the window? That is so it can get the full benefit of the sun.

What a picture of Christians, who look to Jesus, the Light of the world! (John 8:12). The Lord gives His energy—His starch, or strength, and His sugar, or sweetness. Lovingly He invites us who love Him to help ourselves to His strength and sweetness. And that's how we develop Christ-like characters, which the Bible calls the fruit of the Spirit—love, joy, peace, longsuffering, gentleness, goodness, faith, meekness, and temperance (or self-control), (Gal. 5:22, 23).

Leaves themselves don't have the power to stop producing fruit. They work for the tree automatically. But that's one way in which your life is different from that of a leaf. You have the power to choose whether or not you'll bear fruit. You can say "No" to the Lord and not bear His fruit of love, joy, peace, and the rest of the Christian virtues that God wants every Christian to develop. But you'll be much happier and a very much more useful person if you choose to love the Lord, and read and obey His word. Then *He* will see to it that your life will bear sweet fruit for Him and your Christ-like influence will attract others to your Saviour.

God's Word, A Plumb Line

THEME   The importance of lining up with God's Word.

MATERIALS   A piece of white string, with a weight hanging on the end, thus making a home-made plumb line.

CAN you guess what object is found in nearly every home and in almost every kind of store, something which comes in different colors and different thicknesses or weights, sometimes used in the spring by boys for flying kites and spinning tops and by girls who play with a yo-yo? There! You all know the answer now, don't you? Yes, it is *string* [show a piece].

But not only can we have fun with string—it has some important uses, too. String is useful for more than tying up packages. Did you know that it is actually used in constructing large buildings? Did you ever hear of a plumb line? This is a piece of string with a weight on the end of it [let your plumb line hang down] that is hung down beside the walls of a building, to check whether it is being built straight. Plumb lines were used in Bible days, nearly 800 years before Christ was born (Amos 7:7, 8).

Suppose some men would figure that if they'd work hard, and do the best they could, they wouldn't need a plumb line. Would the wall they were erecting be perfectly straight? No contractor would want his workmen to build a wall in that haphazard way.

The builders might argue with the contractor that they built the wall very carefully. They might insist that it was straight. But a plumb line could be rigged up and the crookedness of the walls would be proved by the vertical string, which would hang straight down. The builders could become angry and tear down the string; they might cut it up or burn it. But their anger would not straighten the wall. The wall's crookedness would not be the fault of the string—the string would simply point out the builders' errors.

The workmen would be foolish to be angry at the string or plumb line, wouldn't they? Yet, boys and girls, that same thing happens over and over again—not with a plumb line and buildings, but with people and the eternal Word of God. For the Bible can be likened to string. It can be enjoyed by boys and girls, as you enjoy playing games with string. But, more important, it can enable you to build your life straight and strong. If you know God's Word well, and obey God's orders in it, you will be kept from sin (Ps. 119:11). Like a plumb line, God's Word will line up your life in such a way that you will be as a beautiful temple or building of honor for the Lord.

To have a plumb line and not to follow its guidance would be completely foolish. So also, to have God's Word and not to follow its teachings, is foolishness. When a workman sees that a brick wall is out of line, he changes the crooked bricks, not the true plumb line.

But when God's Word reveals men's hearts in all their wrong leanings and crookedness, they usually hate the Word and refuse to hear it (John 3:19-21).

But when you or someone else receives the Word and follows its instruction, God helps you to correct your crooked ways. You accomplish nothing by becoming angry at God's Word when it shows you your sin and mistakes. For centuries, men have tried to destroy the Bible for that very reason—but no one has ever succeeded. God's Word will stand forever. You can't change His Word—it's much better to change your life, by believing in God's Son.

Cities have building inspectors whose business it is to check on new and old buildings. Do you think they would approve a building whose walls lean at angles? No, they would order, "Tear it down!" To have the approval of the Chief Inspector, the Lord Jesus, we must line up our lives with His true Word. For no matter how hard we try, how many good things we do, or how carefully we work, our lives can never be what God wants them to be without His help. The Bible is the one true and final line by which our lives will be judged (John 12:48).

(Omit the next illustration if your time is short and conclude with the last paragraph.)

George Washington Carver, the great scientist, felt that nothing should ever be wasted. He even made it a habit to save every little piece of string he found. Once he picked up a piece of string and felt something strange on it. He checked closely and found that on the string was a bit of mold. Mold, you know, is a growth which appears on damp or decaying articles. Have you ever seen moldy bread or cheese?

Most people would have thrown the moldy string away, but Mr. Carver investigated it carefully and discovered that this type of mold could destroy vast amounts of cotton. He not only found out the destructiveness of the mold, but also found a way to fight it.

We should treasure or save up every verse, every portion of God's Word. Mr. Carver prevented tragedy to the cotton industry by saving a little piece of string. You can avoid sin and the tragedy it brings by hiding God's Word in your heart. Sometimes you may feel that it isn't important to listen to your Sunday School teacher or Junior Church leader, or that you don't have to obey every single word of the Bible. But you will save yourself from great loss if you will treasure and live by all of God's Word.

Mr. Carver needed a great deal of wisdom and scientific knowledge to be able to prepare a remedy to destroy that mold. We too, need a thorough knowledge of the Bible if we are to fight sin.

Have you lined up your life by the true Word of God? When it points out that you are leaning the wrong way, do you become angry—or do you ask the Lord to correct your crookedness? In Matthew 22:29, Jesus tells us one reason why men err or sin—they do not know the Scriptures. Let's study our Sunday School lessons and read our Bibles every day, so that we will know the Scriptures and let them teach us how to live for God.

Without Spot or Wrinkle

THEME Keeping clean and unspotted as Christians.

MATERIALS Three cotton handkerchiefs (preferably men's): one spotted with dirt and stained in the middle with fruit juice, coffee or something else that noticeably stains; one washed but not ironed; one ironed. Bottle labeled "spot remover"; soap (or soap powder); an electric iron.
(If you are using this object lesson on a week day instead of Sunday, you may want to actually wash the soiled handkerchief and iron the wrinkled one as you speak of them.) Have pupils who read well be prepared to read Isaiah 43:7, 21; I John 1:9; and the last sentence of Revelation 1:5.

LET'S read a verse of Scripture, Ephesians 5:27. (Read this verse, substituting "Christians" for each "it.") What do you think the Lord means by Christians being presented to Him some day without a spot or wrinkle?

If someone would offer to loan you a handkerchief like this [show soiled one], would you want to use it? Do you think the Governor of our State or the President of the United States would want to use it? No, they would be insulted if you'd offer it to them. Why would they be insulted—because this handkerchief is made of cotton, or because it is only part linen? No, they wouldn't want it because it is *dirty*—it is spotted and full of blemishes. What are blemishes? Yes, they are stains. Do you think that if we'd fold this handkerchief so that the dirt spots and stains wouldn't show, it would be all right? [Do this.] Would you want to use it now? No, it's still dirty and stained. It must have the spots removed and be washed clean before anyone would want to use it.

In some ways we Christians are like this handkerchief. Was this manufactured, or made, for a definite use? How about us? Did God create us for His definite use? Don, will you read Isaiah 43, verses 7 and 21?

God distinctly tells us that He created us for the purpose of not only being a help and a blessing to others, but to live such godly lives that we'll show forth His glories and attractiveness and bring Him pleasure by attracting others to Him (Rev. 4:11b).

But we disappoint the Lord. We don't give His Word a chance to change our naturally sinful hearts. And so we become spotted, perhaps even stained, with sin—we are no longer useful to the Lord. Perhaps we try to fold our sins under, and cover them up, as we tried to do with the dirt and stains in the handkerchief. But the Lord sees everything we do—He knows even our most secret thoughts! (Ps. 139: 1-12.) If we are ever to be of service to the Lord, we must keep clean. How can we do that? By telling the Lord we are sorry and that we honestly want to quit sinning. If we confess our sins to God in this spirit, what will He do? Ted, read I John 1:9, please. How thankful we can be that the Lord will forgive us and cleanse us if we mean business with Him!

To make this soiled and stained handkerchief clean, we must remove its stains either with boiling water or with the special spot-remover that will take away these particular stains [hold up bottle labeled "spot remover"], and we must thoroughly wash it with water and soap [hold up or point to soap]. Will just bringing this handkerchief *near* the spot remover and soap [do this] be enough? No, we must *apply* the spot remover and wash the handkerchief *in* soapy water.

What is the only thing that will remove our sin-spots and wash us clean? Tom can tell us from Revelation 1:5 (last sentence). Only the blood of Christ! God counts Christ's blood, which He shed on the cross long ago, our sin-remover today. Aren't you glad that you can learn

27

about having your sins cleansed right here at Sunday School (or whatever meeting you are conducting)?

Now suppose that we have removed the stains and washed our soiled handkerchief clean. It looks like this [show clean, unironed handkerchief]. But before this handkerchief is ready for use, what must we do to it? Yes, iron it. [Point to iron.] Before we iron it, we must sprinkle it [illustrate], so that it will be easy to iron.

The heat in this electric iron and the pressure applied remove the wrinkles. Then we fold the handkerchief and iron it again [fold handkerchief in half]—we fold it and iron it again and again [demonstrate]. Each time we fold it, it looks smaller. Now it is ready to be used. As we Christians more and more obey all the Scripture we read and learn to know, the Holy Spirit of God works in our lives, causing us to want our way less and less, and God's way more and more. Then our selfish natures become smaller and smaller. And the smaller and more humble we become, the more ready we are for God to use us.

Now let's all read Ephesians 5:27 together again. Can you remember to put in the word "Christians" instead of each "it"? [Have group read.] The Lord Jesus longs to have all of us who believe in Him "a glorious church." He will do His part in taking away all our sin-spots and selfish wrinkles if we'll do ours—ask Him every day to keep us clean and to give us strength to stay away from everything that we know He wouldn't approve. As we pray now, tell the Lord that you desire to be clean and useful for Him.

Seeds of Blessing

THEME God's Word will last forever.

MATERIALS On one saucer, an apple cut in half; on another saucer, seeds which you have removed from the fruit. Hold saucers before the group, one in each hand.

IF YOU had the choice of the fruit on this saucer [extend saucer] or the seeds on this other saucer [extend it], which would you choose? Will John and Mary please come here? Which would you choose, John? Which would you choose, Mary? [Let the children take their choices.] You both prefer the fruit over the seeds. Why? You say that the fruit tastes better? Do the rest of you agree with John and Mary?

Suppose that they had chosen the seeds. What use could they have made of them? Yes, plant them. If they were careful to plant the seeds in the right soil and climate and would give the seedling trees the care they would need, in about six or eight years they would have not just one apple, but bushels of them.

But you say, "It is too long to wait. I would rather have one apple right now than wait six or eight years to have bushels."

A young lady in California once bought a piece of property and planted some fruit trees on it. An elderly lady who had owned property there for years asked, "Why are you doing that? It takes so long to raise fruit trees. You'll never enjoy the fruit."

The young lady replied, "Someone will." Years slipped by and the trees began to bear lovely, juicy peaches. This same elderly lady lived long enough to enjoy eating delicious fruit from those trees.

She admitted, "How foolish I've been! I, too, could have had trees bearing fruit—I could have had all I wanted and given some to my neighbors—but foolishly, I never planted a tree! I thought fruit trees would take so long to bear that I wouldn't bother with them. But these last few years, since the trees were planted, have gone so fast that I can hardly believe it."

Many folks today are interested only in things that they can enjoy *now*. Their chief concern is making themselves happy at the present time. They don't care about God's long range plan, what He wants them to do during their lifetime, or how He wants them to prepare for the next life. They are not interested in the Word of God which would interest them in lasting things. They refuse to think of where they'll live forever and ever, in eternity. They live only for today.

Many boys and girls, and even some grownups, don't come to church to learn from God's Word about the long, long life they'll live after this short one. They come to church just to have a good time. When their pastor preaches the Word of God, which Jesus said is like *seed,* because it produces fruit in the hearts of those who take it in, they talk, or laugh, or write notes. They are at Sunday School or Church only to meet friends and to enjoy themselves. They have never really learned to love the Lord or to enjoy His Word. Sometimes even Christians fail to realize the great privilege they have of studying the Word of God in a church where the Gospel is preached. Their minds, too, are only on what they like to do today. They don't realize that the Lord compares our time on earth to a puff of wind (Job 7:7), and that our life with Him in heaven will never, never end. That is what "everlasting" means in John 3:16, a verse which we all know.

There wasn't enough fruit in that one apple which I brought this morning to let you all have some. There was just enough for John and Mary to enjoy. But suppose that six or eight years ago some other class had had the same choice put up to them that you had this morning and they had chosen to plant the seeds in our own church yard (or some other appropriate spot). By now there would have been enough apples for all of us to enjoy.

We *can* count the seeds in an apple, but we *can't* count the apples that are in one seed. What does this mean? An apple tree may grow from a single seed. And we cannot know how many apples one tree will bear— how many bushels year after year.

Did you ever hear of Johnny Appleseed? He was an American pioneer who traveled hundreds of miles, about the year 1800, through Pennsylvania, Ohio, and Indiana, wearing a coffee sack for a shirt and a saucepan for a hat, and carrying a Bible and a package of apple seeds. Can you picture him walking barefoot over the country (remember, there were few roads in those days), planting and pruning thousands of apple trees as he walked along? For many years after Johnny Appleseed died, those apple trees were bearing fruit. Each apple was a reminder of the thoughtfulness of this man.

Suppose Johnny Appleseed had said, "What's the use of my planting apple seeds all over this country? Maybe eight years from now I'll be dead. I won't get to enjoy those apples"? If he had thought only of himself and his own enjoyment at that time, think of how much fruit would never have been borne and enjoyed by countless hungry boys and girls and fathers and mothers. No, Johnny Appleseed was thinking ahead and he was also thinking of others.

You boys and girls may think, "Why should I study my Sunday School lesson every day and do my homework for school and help Mom? I could be having a good time!" These important duties are like planting seeds. In their right time they'll bear fruit—and it will be much sooner than you'd think. Time *does* march on!

Since the average time for an apple tree to bear fruit is only around 30 years, it reminds us that things on this earth do not last very long. What is the only thing that will last forever? Ann, please read what God says to us in

31

Matthew 24:35—"Heaven and earth shall pass away, but my words shall not pass away." Since God's Book is the only thing that will last forever, we know that it is vitally important for us to know and appreciate the Bible.

Let us pray now that we shall daily plant the kind of seeds that will bear fruit and bring blessing to many others. Also let's ask the Lord to help us more and more *love* God's Word, and *learn* God's Word, and *live* God's Word.

Coal, Moth Balls, and Perfume

THEME   Refined Christians.

MATERIALS   As many of the following as you can get: lump of coal; moth balls; bottle of perfume; record player and a phonograph record of a Gospel song; a bottle of bleach; anything plastic; nylon cord, hose, or other clothing; a lead pencil; aspirin; sulfa tablet; saccharine; creosote. (Bottles labeled with the names of the last four by-products of coal may be used if you don't have the originals.)

ALL of you recognize what this is. [Hold up a piece of coal.] Thousands of years ago, this coal was not black and hard as it is now, but it was green. It was made up of fern leaves or trees or bushes that lived in the sunshine and enjoyed fresh air. What happened to change it so? For many years storms beat, winds blew, rains came, floods swept over the earth. And the ferns, trees, grasses, and shrubs became covered with sand, clay, and dirt. They were pressed down, down, buried under many millions of pounds of pressure, for years and years. There the dead plants received no light, no life, no sunshine. That is the history of this piece of coal.

And, strangely enough, that is the history of all people, too. Adam and Eve, the first man and woman on earth, lived, walked, talked, and enjoyed the beautiful Garden of Eden, were blessed with the fellowship of God and felt the warmth of His presence. They would talk with God in the cool of the evening. But one day Adam and Eve sinned by disobeying God. God then had to drive them out of the beautiful garden and from the sunshine of His love. They were weighed down under the terrible burden of their sin.

And for over 6,000 years since then, men and women and boys and girls have, like Adam and Eve, sinned against God, and have been burdened by the weight of their sins.

It was many centuries ago when men first discovered coal. They found some pieces lying on the ground, and noticed that these black lumps burned hotter and longer than wood. Later men began to dig, or mine this important fuel. Sometimes they went down into the earth at great danger to themselves, working even in water. Though cold and uncomfortable, they endured all these privations to bring up coal, for coal would bring warmth and blessing to their homes and the homes of others. That's why someone has called coal "buried sunshine." It would have stayed buried if men hadn't lifted it up and brought it out.

Isn't all this a picture of us? We were buried under the burden of sin but were found by Jesus, God's Son. Jesus left heaven, came into this world of sin, suffered hardships, pain, and even death. He willingly became poor in order that we might be made rich with His gifts of salvation, power, and love (II Cor. 8:9). Why did Jesus do all this? Yes, He wants to lift, or save, us from our sins. Besides lifting us from *our* sins, He wants us to show others how Jesus can lift them from their sins. In this way we can help to bring God's warmth and life to those who need it.

You may say, "We don't burn coal at our house, so we don't need it—coal isn't a blessing to us!" Perhaps you don't know that coal is refined and made into things that you do use. From pieces of coal like this [display it again], come things that you need and use day after day.

Here is a bag of moth balls [show]. How white and different these marble-size moth balls look when I hold them beside this piece of black coal. Yet they are taken from coal. They are what chemists call a by-product of coal. Moth balls are coal that is refined, or perfected.

34

They have within them something that prevents moths from ruining woolen garments.

Do you know that a Christian boy or girl or man or woman who loves the Lord Jesus Christ can keep others from having their lives ruined by little sins? If *you* don't laugh at unclean jokes or stories, if you do not cheat, or steal or lie—and if you *do* live to please Jesus day by day—others won't want to do evil things when you're around. Though many won't agree with you, they will respect you for taking your stand as a Christian.

We can't stop destructive moths with a piece of coal, but refined coal will stop those dangerous insects. So let's learn a lesson from coal and allow the Lord to teach us more and more after we're saved, and thus refine us. Let's listen to our pastor, the evangelist, or our Sunday School teacher. Let's obey all the truth we know so that we'll be better Christians, and will know how to help others as we have been helped.

Do you like to hear good Gospel records? (If you have a record player, play part of a record. If not, simply hold up a record.) Do you know that phonograph records are also made from coal? Yes, they're another by-product. We'd be silly to try to play this piece of coal on a record player, because the coal itself hasn't a message. But *refined* coal, made into a record, can and does carry a message. The record becomes a witness for the Lord.

You girls will be interested in this [show perfume]. What a lovely fragrance we enjoy when we remove the cap from this bottle of perfume! Perfume is another by-product of coal. Some Christians seem to carry a sweet fragrance of heaven wherever they go. And everyone knows it—others can tell that they have been with Jesus. Their songs, their testimonies, their lives are so Christ-like that they seem to have the odor of heavenly perfume. How different they are from those who lie, say unkind words, tell unclean stories, and do every sort of thing that isn't at all like Jesus! By comparison, such lives smell like a garbage pail. Don't you want to be a sweet-smelling Christian?

Sometimes, when folks are quite sick the doctor gives them a sulfa drug [show this] to break up the infection. Did you know that sulfa drugs, as well as aspirins [show these] are also made from coal? We who are God's children can be used as healing medicines to those who are sin-sick, without hope in the Lord. That is, we can help people if we'll only let the Lord refine us through His Word and prayer and discipline. A piece of coal cannot stop a headache or an infection—it must first be refined. God gives us His Word, teachers, pastors, and evangelists to perfect us so that we can be used for Him (Eph. 4:11, 12).

Here are some other things made from coal—bleach, which takes away stubborn stains; nylon, which is used not only in making hosiery and other clothing [show these] but also for parachutes and cords that have to be extra strong; creosote, that keeps termites and rot from destroying lumber; saccharine, to sweeten tea and coffee for folks who can't eat sugar; graphite, the part of the pencil which makes the marks on paper. These are just a few of the goodlooking and useful things that are made from dirty pieces of coal.

If *men* can make such a variety of useful things from lumps of black coal, just think what God can do with, and for, all those who let Him not only save them, but allow Him to *refine* them! God can make you a wonderful blessing to many, if you'll ask Him, and believe with all your heart that He will.

However, there are some boys and girls—and grown-ups too— who are satisfied with barely being lifted out of the pit of sin. They are satisfied merely to be unrefined, lump-of-coal Christians. They don't seem to realize that God must punish sin, even when the sinner is a Christian. Our holy, righteous God hates all sin, and He wants His children to hate it too.

The only way you can keep from sinning is to love

and obey God's Word, let God refine you and keep ridding you of any sinful desires. As He more and more refines you, you'll bring warmth, sweetness, health, and blessing to those around you who greatly need the Lord. God's promise is that His eyes are over the righteous, and His ears are open to their prayers, but His warning is that His face is against them that do evil (I Pet. 3:12). Let's bow our heads now in silent prayer. Each one tell the Lord what you want to be—only a lump-of-coal Christian, or a refined, blessing-filled Christian.

Melody In the Heart

THEME Jesus' joyful melody for discordant hearts.

MATERIALS This object lesson may be illustrated either on the blackboard, a large sheet of paper, or on a flannelboard. If you use a blackboard or paper, draw a heart, music notes, and cross, as shown in Sketch 1, as each is called for in your message. If you want to show what gifts of the Lord Jesus cause a Christian's heart to sing, write the 12 gifts of the Lord Jesus, as you mention them, inside the music notes.

If you use a flannelboard, make an outline heart as large as possible, of red bias tape or yarn on your flannelboard, pinning it in place. Make 7 white music notes and 5 black ones; also, a cross, to be placed within the heart, and backed with flannel or suede scraps so that they will adhere to the board. Prepare word-cards, rounded at the top, to apply with Scotch tape on each music note (see Sketch 2). As you mention each gift, simply flap the right word-card over its note. Also have ready a tin pan. If you are using a flannelboard,

Spiritual "Shoes" That Fit

THEME Growing spiritually as God has purposed.

MATERIALS A very small pair of baby shoes; a larger pair; a pair of women's high-heel shoes; a pair of men's shoes.

HERE'S a riddle. What have eyes but cannot see; tongues, but can't talk; and soles, but can't go to heaven? Yes, shoes!

Why do you wear shoes? That's right, you wear them to protect your feet and to help you to get around better on rough ground. How many of you ever walk around barefoot outside? Did you ever bruise a toe, or step on a bee, or cut your foot? Yes, you can really hurt your feet when you don't wear shoes.

Shoes themselves do not enable us to walk, run, jump, play, or work. No, we have to have *feet* inside our shoes, and *life* in our feet, before we can do any walking, running or jumping. But when you walk into our classroom, and I look at you, I do not see bare feet. Neither do I think especially of the life that is in your feet. But I do notice your *shoes*.

Shoes, then, remind us of a Christian's walk, or behavior, which everyone sees. People do not see you when you're having your daily devotions—reading your Bible and praying. But they do see you as you walk to and from school and church and with your friends. They see the way you act and the things you do.

Who could wear shoes like this? [Hold up baby shoes.] Yes, a small baby. And shoes like this? [Hold up men's shoes.] What are some differences between these two pairs of shoes? Yes, the color. What else? Size—yes, and what makes the big difference in size? Why do men's shoes have to be so large? Because there are years of growth between a baby's foot and a man's foot. In Luke 2:40 we read that the Boy Jesus grew in stature, which means that He grew taller and bigger year by year. You are all growing too, month by month and year by year. That's natural, but did you know that God also expects you to grow spiritually? Jesus grew in favor with God as well as in height and weight. Peter and Alex, will you please read some other Scripture verses which show that God wants His children to grow up spiritually? (Have boys read II Peter 3:18 and Ephesians 4:15.)

God *expects* us to grow. He expects us to study His Word and to love and enjoy it, just as much as we enjoy the food we eat every day. If we do, we shall just naturally grow and develop—not all in a day, a week or a month, but little by little. As we do, we shall be carrying out the purpose for which the Lord placed each one of us on earth. God has put you in the very family and town where He wants you to be.

As a baby grows, the time comes when he learns to walk. His wearing a pair of walking shoes is no guarantee that he can walk. His muscles and mind must have developed so that walking becomes the natural thing for him to do. It's true that his parents put sturdy shoes on him, but the shoes themselves can't make their baby walk.

If we who are Christians will hear, believe, and obey God's Word, we shall grow spiritually. Soon our walk will show others that we love the Lord.

How would you like to try to wear these small shoes? (Let some older child attempt to try on the larger pair of baby shoes.) No, they won't fit. Did you girls ever pretend you were grown-up ladies and wear your mother's high heels? (Let a girl put on the high heeled shoes and walk in them.) Clump, clump, clump. What a noise you make—and if you wear them very long your feet surely

44

will hurt. Why? The shoes aren't the right size! Yet there are some boys and girls, and men and women too, who try to wear spiritual shoes that belong to a Sunday School teacher or their pastor or someone else. Sometimes they wear these wrong shoes for a long time—so long, in fact, that their feet get sore and they become discouraged and say, "I can't be a good Christian; it's too hard." Their trouble results from trying to wear someone else's shoes, that don't fit them.

Perhaps you will understand this better if I tell you a story. Someone says, "Come on Jim, let's go in back of the garage and have a smoke."

Jim answers, "My pastor doesn't believe in that. My Sunday School teacher says it is wrong. My church doesn't think it's right to do such things." Jim is not standing on his *own* testimony—nor in his *own* shoes.

Jim should answer, "Since I am a Christian and want to serve the Lord, I cannot do those things, for His Word says not to love the world and its sinful pleasures (I John 2:15). God also tells me to keep away from all appearances of evil (I Thess. 5:22). No, I don't do such things because the Lord Jesus has given me something much better."

If Jim would say this, he would be standing in his *own* shoes. After all, if we don't do things just because our church, our pastor, or our Sunday School teacher doesn't believe in them, we'll have a mighty clumpety, clumpety, clumpety, walk—we'll be playing dress-up and we won't fool anyone. All of you can tell when a little girl is playing "dress-up" by her uneven, stumbling walk. And folks can tell by your walk whether you have grown up spiritually or if you are just trying to pretend that you're grown.

God's Word tells us that though the Children of Israel wandered for 40 years through a sandy and rocky wilderness, their shoes didn't wear out, nor did their feet swell (Deut. 29:5; Neh. 9:21). God miraculously took care of their shoes. He made them fit and kept them from wearing out. God also will keep our "conduct shoes," our testimony, from wearing out, if we keep walking by faith and in love as He tells us to (II Cor. 5:7; Eph. 5:2).

You probably know that it used to be a custom in China to bind tightly the feet of baby girls born into rich families. As a result their feet were kept from growing normally. The Chinese thought that small feet were a sign of beauty and wealth. But the girls with bound feet never could walk properly.

Satan, the enemy of all Christians, would like to do something like that to all boys and girls who trust in the Lord Jesus. He wants to keep you from ever being able to walk before the world with a straightforward testimony for Christ. Satan tries to bind you with the fear of being laughed at—or of not having fun—or of not being popular, and oh, many other things, until you get discouraged and neglect your daily reading of God's Word. But if you refuse to listen to Satan and faithfully trust and obey the Lord, He will help you to "walk worthy" of Him (Col. 1:10) and to carry out the purpose for which He made you. As I say (or sing) the words of the chorus of *Walking with Jesus** tell the Lord whether this is your testimony, too.

"I'd rather walk with Jesus than roam the paths of sin,
I'd rather have His friendship than earth's best honors win;
My one desire to please Him as daily ways we trod
And so we're walking onward, upward, bound for heaven
—*and God!*"

* Copyright, 1930, by C. Harold Lowden. Used by permission.

Lifeless Dolls or the Living Saviour?

THEME Heaven and hell.

MATERIALS Many types, sizes, and kinds of dolls, such as rag, paper, rubber, storybook dolls, old and new dolls. The week before this lesson ask the girls to bring their favorite and unusual dolls. The dolls will create interest, and will make an attractive display.

THANK you, girls, for bringing your dolls. [Comment on the kinds of dolls and anything outstanding about them.]

How do these dolls differ from each other? [Let the girls briefly explain the apparent differences.] Yes, these dolls are very different, yet they are alike in one way— they are all lifeless. It's true that some of them look extremely life-like and alive. Some of these dolls (or dolls in the store) have life-like skin, hair that you girls can wash and comb—they can cry tears, walk, and even say a word or two. But in spite of their having all these life-like traits, they are not alive.

About how long ago, do you suppose, were dolls first made, and of what materials were they made? If you are ever in London, England, you may see in the British Museum there some of the oldest dolls known. Some were made in Egypt and were carved from thin boards something like canoe paddles. Thus they are called "paddle dolls." Their clothes are simply carved lines, and their hair is made of beads. Ancient Greek and Roman dolls are also in the museum. Some were made of wood, and some of clay. None of those ancient dolls look like any of the dolls we have here today.

Do you boys think it's sissified to be interested in

dolls? You'll be surprised to know that those Egyptian and Greek dolls we have been talking about were not made for little girls, nor were they made to play with. They were made for grown men and women, especially for kings, who were called Pharaohs in Egypt, and for other rich and prominent men and women. Do you wonder why those grownups had dolls made for them? It was for the express purpose of being *buried* with those great folks when they died! Those ancient heroes supposed that the dolls would be their friends and servants in the land of death, and would help, encourage, and protect them. The Egyptians had their paddle dolls made with no feet or legs so that they couldn't run away from their dead masters!

You probably are thinking, "That's silly, dolls are lifeless—they can't be any company, let alone be of any help!" You're right, but those people didn't know and love God and so were basing all their hopes on their own superstitious ideas. There is something about the uncertainties of death which troubles men and women, even though they may be rich and famous. They feel a strong need of something or someone to help them and to make them brave when they're about to die.

They did not know, as you do, that all those who love and trust Jesus as their Saviour go to be with Him as soon as they die. To make this fact clear, the Bible tells us that for Christians to be "absent from the body" is to be "present with the Lord." You all know what it means to be *absent* or *present* in school or Sunday School. When a person dies, his real self is absent from his body. His body is buried in the ground. But his real self, or soul, as we call it, goes at once to be with Jesus if he is a believer. He cannot go to be with Jesus if he is not a believer. Jesus can accept for heaven only those who have accepted Him on earth. While Jesus was preaching on earth, He spoke much about life after death. He pictured the hope of heaven and the fear of death.

People don't like to think about hell. They argue

that because God is loving and patient, He won't send anyone to hell. It's true that God doesn't *want* anyone to go there (II Pet. 3:9b). In Old Testament days God sent one prophet after another to warn His people to turn from their evil ways to the great God who loved them and longed for them to be saved. But very few people listened to the prophets. Finally God sent His own Son, the Lord Jesus, to earth.

Jesus came from heaven and knew how wonderful it is. When Jesus was about to go back to heaven, He told His disciples that He was going to prepare and reserve places for them and all others who would believe that He came to save them and give them eternal life (John 14:2).

Jesus also knew that the heavenly Father has a place prepared and reserved for all who will not believe in Him (Jude 13). The Bible calls this place hell. Jesus often spoke about it and warned over and over that unless people would believe that He is THE Way (the one and only way) to His Father and heaven (John 14:6), they would go to that awful place.

God's Word is plain. God has sent His Son to be the Saviour of the world. Everyone who has *asked* God's Son to be his own personal Saviour has eternal life . . . that means he has Jesus as his Friend and Companion and Helper and Protector now on this earth and he will have Him for ever and ever in heaven. How much more wonderful to have God's own living Son than a lifeless doll!

Because of this, we who are trusting in the Lord Jesus don't have to be afraid, and can say when we are going through what we call "the valley of the shadow of death," "We will fear no evil," knowing that we "will dwell in the house of the Lord forever" (Ps. 23:4, 6).

Let us praise the Lord now that our trust is not in any lifeless doll that cannot hear us, or love us back, but our trust is in our loving Saviour who is living now at His Father's right hand, praying for all of us who are His children (Rom. 8:34).

Needful Nails

THEME Necessity of humility of Christ's witness.

MATERIALS Several nails of different sizes; a hammer; a small board in which to drive nails; your coat.

W HAT important lessons can we learn from this common nail? Nails are made to do definite jobs, such as joining boards together or holding pictures or other articles on our walls. Their jobs are humble, yet they are important and necessary.

Christians, too, have definite jobs, and they are similar to those of nails. You—if you're a Christian—are to join certain things together. You are also to be a burden-bearer, much as a nail supports what is hung on it.

One of the many things to which the Bible compares the Lord Jesus is "a nail in a sure place" (Isa. 22:23). We who are Christians want to be like Jesus in every way we can. How can we be like a nail? How can we Christians hold things together? How can we bear burdens? How can we make shaky and wobbly things steady and sure?

Suppose we let this nail suggest answers to our questions. This nail has a head. What is the head for? Yes, to be struck or driven by a hammer. If we think of a nail's representing a Christian, a hammer can represent the Word of God. Long years ago, God said through one of His faithful prophets, "Is not my word like . . . a hammer?" (Jer. 23:29). Yes, God's Word is sometimes a hammer to pound on hard hearts. Did you ever hear or read a part of God's Word which seemed to pound on your heart and persuade and encourage you to do what's right?

But for a nail to do its work effectively, it must have not only a head, but a point. The point helps the nail to penetrate wood without splitting it. Christians, of all people, have a point in life, a definite reason for living. The Apostle Paul said, "For to me to live is Christ" (Phil. 1:21). The reason, or point, of Paul's life, then, was to live as the Lord Jesus directed him and to point others to Him.

Between the head and the point of each nail is a strong backbone, the part the carpenter holds when he starts pounding. This backbone, or shaft, of a nail is what holds things together. It reminds us of the will, or power of choice, of Christians. This shaft must be strong enough to stand up under the power which the hammer-like Word of God brings down on it, until it joins what a Christian knows he *ought* to do with what he *wants* to do. Rebekah said, "I *will* go" to be Isaac's wife (Gen. 24:58). Joshua said, "We *will* serve the Lord" (Josh. 24:15). The prodigal son, after realizing how foolish he had been to leave his father's home, said, "I *will* arise and go to my father" (Luke 15:18). We thank God that each of these had a *will* to follow the Lord.

When nails keep bending as we drive them, they are impossible to use. Let's not collapse, but go on and let God's Word drive us into the special place of service where He wants us to be.

You can tap a nail lightly into a board with a hammer [do this], and it may *look* as though it's anchored firmly in that board. But see what happens when you hang something on that nail, like this coat! [Coat falls to floor.] The nail has not had enough of the hammer's compelling force behind it. Have you ever hung something on a loose nail? Did you like it when the nail came out and your coat fell on the floor? Of course not!

That makes us wonder how many times we have failed the Lord because we have not let the hammer of God's Word drive us into our place for Him.

In our church we have only [give number] pianos.

We don't have many rooms—we can easily count them. We may be proud of our organ, but there is only one in the whole church. These are big things, that stand out. But how many nails do you think are in this building? No doubt thousands! It's true that nails aren't prominent, they're not outstanding. Yet many nails were needed and were important in constructing this building.

In Old Testament days "David prepared iron in abundance for the nails" to be used by his son Solomon in building the magnificent temple (I Chron. 22:3). As hundreds of nails are required in building each room in a church like ours, so God has need of many, many "nail-Christians." Yes, most Christians are not prominent, or outstanding. But, like nails, we are important as we work together. Without the many nail-Christians there would be no outstanding testimony in any church group, any more than we would have this building without nails.

You may say, "I'm not important—I can't do anything unusual." Let me read you a famous little saying that shows just how important was one nail in a horse's shoe, during a battle of long ago when men fought on horse-

> "For want of a nail, the shoe was lost;
> For want of a shoe, the horse was lost;
> For want of a horse, the rider was lost;
> For want of a rider, the battle was lost;
> For want of a battle, a kingdom was lost;
> And all for the want of a nail!"

If you are a Christian, the Lord wants you to point others to Him. But you can't very well teach others about your humble Lord if you act like a know-it-all, a big shot. To be humble is the opposite of being proud. John the Baptist had the secret of being a successful servant of Jesus. John humbly said of Jesus, "He must *increase*, but I must *decrease*" (John 3:30). By this, John meant that he was willing to be a humble nail-Christian so that the Lord could have all the glory and credit. Shall we pray that this will be our desire too?

Wormy-Apple Christians

THEME The power of Jesus' blood to cleanse sinful hearts.

MATERIALS A large apple, should have inconspicuous worm hole[s], be shined to look pretty; also a knife.

HERE is a nice, large apple. Isn't it a beauty? Someone has well said, "An apple can be enjoyed by all of our five senses." We *see* its beauty; we *smell* its fragrance; we *feel* its firmness; we *hear* its crispy crunch as we bite into its storehouse of vitamins; and we *taste* its juicy flavor.

But in order to share this apple, it must be cut. Jack, will you take this knife and cut the apple in half, so that we can both enjoy it?

My, look at that! You don't want to eat a wormy apple like that, do you, Jack? Neither do I! And yet the outside was so red and shiny and it looked so good—but when Jack cut it open, all of you could see how rotten it is on the inside.

Let's think of this apple as representing people who are trying to *act* like Christians, but whose hearts inside are not changed by the great Life-changer, the Lord Jesus Christ. The knife will represent God's Word. The Bible, you know, likens itself to a sharp two-edged sword (Heb. 4: 12), and a knife is much like a small sword. The true condition of the apple was not revealed or understood by us until the knife cut through to the apple's core or heart, and revealed its inner rottenness. True, the apple was bright and shiny on the outside—it looked as if we could enjoy it—but its heart was disagreeable and bad.

God's Word has a name for people like that, people who try to act as if they love God and hate sin, but who really have never trusted Jesus to cleanse their hearts and make them new and different inside. Jesus called such people *hypocrites* (Matt. 23:25-28). A religious hypocrite tries to act like, talk like, and be like a genuine Christian, but he has never let his heart be changed by Christ.

We would not have discovered what was on the inside of the apple if we had not used the knife. Can you imagine this apple saying, "No one will ever know how rotten my heart is! After all, I look about as good as any of the other apples"? But right here, before all of us, the true condition of this apple has been revealed. The knife showed what was not noticeable before. Just so, God's Word, the Bible, causes those who read it sincerely, to see themselves as they really are *inside,* not outwardly where people see them. God's Word says, "Man looketh on the outward appearance, but the Lord looketh on the heart" (I Sam. 16:7).

Do you know that some day God will reveal before everyone the true condition of your heart? John 12:48 tells us that at that time the Lord Jesus will judge us by God's words. Then the inmost secrets of our hearts will be revealed (Rom. 2:16). In other words, it will be as if a knife is cutting open our hearts, our inner thoughts.

God wants to give new hearts and clean hearts to those who don't know Him, causing old, selfish desires to pass away and new, God-given desires to take their place (II Cor. 5:17). Human hearts, apart from Christ's changing, are deceitful and even desperately wicked (Jer. 17:9). No matter how much an unbeliever tries to cover up his sin, God will some day reveal his inner sinfulness.

When do you think this apple began to get rotten? It started long before you'd think. Its downfall started early in the spring when the tree was in full bloom. A little codling moth flew around the apple tree, and laid its eggs in the blossom. When the eggs hatched, the larvas or worms found themselves in the very center of the tiny apple. That moth destroyed the apple's heart, though the outside of the fruit did not reveal what had been done.

It was just a *little* codling moth, just a *little* egg, and just a *little* worm that ruined this apple. Orchard owners spend about 30 million dollars a year in fighting these destructive moths.

But as awful as these moths are, they do not compare with the horrible results of sin, and the great price that God paid to fight evil. Yes, the wages of sin is death (Rom. 6:23), and God gave His only Son to die and pay the high price of sin for us (John 3:16).

Sin, like a codling moth, starts in a little way when boys and girls are young. A little lie, a little cheating, or a little unbelief concerning God's Word may be sins that you hardly notice. "It's so little, how can it hurt me?" you may ask. But sin keeps working into one's heart until that heart is defiled, perhaps even rotten, and worthless. And all the while that life might appear innocent to other people.

What will stop the evil work of *codling moths* on apple trees? Three strong solutions of insecticides must be sprayed on the trees at different times, the first before the eggs have hatched. Then the eggs generally die and the worms don't get a chance to begin their destructive work.

What will stop the work of *sin* in your heart? You must have faith that the Lord Jesus can remove your sin and cleanse your sinful heart. Is there any spray powerful enough to prevent even the beginnings of inner rottenness? No man-made spray can do it. The prophet Jeremiah said that even nitre (a strong chemical) and much strong soap can't cleanse wicked hearts (Jer. 2:22). But "the precious blood" of the Lord Jesus can and does (I Pet. 1:19). How can blood shed on a cross about 2000 years ago cleanse our sins today? That blood was precious to God because it was the blood of His own Son and it was powerful enough to save everyone who ever has or ever will believe in Jesus as his Saviour. Let's pray now that we'll all trust in the cleansing, changing power of that precious blood, and be true-to-the-core Christians.

The Strongest Rope in the World

THEME The binding power of God's love.

MATERIALS A short piece of rope; a flannel heart; a 36" piece of red string or yarn to bind across the heart; three small cards with word "love" on them, backed with flannel or suede scraps to adhere to the board.

S TRONG rope can tie the biggest ships to their docks. Rope can also lift tons of cargo on to ships.

A manila rope measuring only an inch and a half around can lift a weight of 2,650 pounds, a little more than the weight of a jeep. (A jeep weighs 2,092 lbs.) A thicker manila rope, seven inches around, can lift 41,000 pounds or 20 jeeps. Think how much weight those ropes that are more than 20 inches around, called cables, can hold! But a certain rope which the Bible talks about, is much stronger than even a 20-inch cable. We'll see why, later.

First, however, let's learn about the three main kinds of rope. One kind is made from fibers attached to the trunk of a tree, another from leaves of another tree, and still another is made from the stalk of a plant. The first, and strongest, rope is *manila* rope. This rope is made from the abaca (ah-bah-kah') tree, which grows in the Philippine Islands. The hard fiber that is made into manila rope comes from the leaf stems of the trunk of this abaca tree. Thus, to make a rope [show a piece of rope] that will take long and hard usage, a tree is cut down and its tiny fibers are twisted together very tightly.

The second kind of rope, *sisal* (si' sal), is made from leaves of the agave (ah-gah'vee) plant. Though its fibers are whiter and shinier than the abaca fibers, they are not so strong.

The third rope is made from the *hemp* plant, that grows from seed in one season. The hemp stalks are cut down and from their fibers hemp rope is made.

The grades and strength of these ropes are more or less determined by the sacrifice that each tree or plant must make in order to produce material for rope. The best rope is made from the abaca tree, which has to be cut down; the next best rope is made from agave leaves which can be cut off; and the third and less strong rope comes from the quickly grown hemp plant. There are other fibres, besides these, used in making rope, but they have less strength and less use.

Now we're ready to consider the strongest rope in the whole world, which is described in the Bible. What is *it* made of? What weight or load can it carry? In Hosea 11:4 we read that God "drew them with cords . . . with bands of love." Would you ever have thought of comparing *love* to *rope,* or *cords?* Surely no mere human being's love could be compared to the strongest of ropes. But God's rope-like love is strong enough to lift the whole world— that is, all men and women and boys and girls who have sunk in the miry clay of sin and despair, who cannot even begin to lift themselves.

God so loved us sinful people *first*—long before we began to love Him (I John 4:19). God loved us "while we were yet sinners" (Rom. 5:8). He sent His own dearly loved Son to take on Himself all our sin, then to take the punishment we deserve. Only the strong rope-like love of God could have made Christ willing to die in our place, to sacrifice His life for ours. An abaca tree has no choice in laying down its life in order that rope might be made. But the Lord Jesus loved us so much that He willingly gave Himself for us (Eph. 5:25b), in order that Christians might be drawn to Him and He might have a Church of believers. And that same rope of love draws men and women to safety in Him, then keeps on holding us securely and helping us to live for Him. God said through His prophet Jeremiah, "Yea, I have loved thee with *an everlasting love;* therefore with lovingkindness have I *drawn* thee" (Jer. 31:3).

One of those who was so drawn to Christ was a Chinese bandit who had been a gambler, a river thief, and a drunkard. After he heard the Gospel of the Lord Jesus Christ and received Him into his heart and life, his whole being was changed. The bad things that he had done before he no longer did. He had been in the habit of beating, cursing, and in every way mistreating his wife. You would think she would have been happy that he had changed so much for the better, but instead she became furious. She swore, beat *him,* and was as disagreeable as she could be. But her Christian husband made no attempt to get even. Then she went on a strike. She would not get out of bed. She would not cook or wash or do any of her household duties. The poor man finally went to the missionary and told him his sad story. He said, "I'll give up being a Christian; there is nothing else I can do."

But the missionary answered, "There is only one thing you need to do. Tie her up with the strongest rope in the world." He told the man that the only rope that would hold her fast was the love of Christ, spoken of in God's Word.

The Chinese decided to try this rope of love [put first *love* card on the heart and string around it, as in the sketch]. On his way home, he bought some meat, though they rarely had meat. He also bought a good piece of cloth for a new dress for his wife. When he got home, he washed the dirty dishes and then cooked dinner. His wife became quite curious about his loving and considerate behavior [put second *love* card on the heart and string around it]. Finally she called out that she was going to get up. But her husband told her that he knew she was tired, and wanted her to rest. She didn't yell at him this time.

Later, when she again wanted to get up, he told her to rest some more, for when she got better she would want to make a new dress. While the wife couldn't understand why her husband was being so kind, the "rope of love" was tying her up tight [put third *love* card on heart and string around it].

When she couldn't stand it any longer, she got up and said, "Go on, study your Bible. It's my work to cook and wash dishes and I don't want you to do it." The next Sunday, when he walked to church, his wife was with him. And before long, that wife accepted the Saviour to whom she had been drawn by the love of her saved husband.

You can influence people too, if you love Jesus and want to reach them for Him. You too can bind their hearts. How? With love, as this heart is bound [point to *love* cards and red string on flannel heart].

Love, the strongest rope in the world, will not only lift your burden of sin if you ask the Lord Jesus to save you, but it will pull you close to Him.

How wonderful to be lifted from sin by God's love! How wonderful, too, to draw others to Jesus by showing forth His love! Let's all thank Him for His great love now by singing with all our hearts, "I Love Him."

Obeying God's Safety Laws

THEME Obedience.

MATERIALS If possible, a rabbit's foot; a four-leaf clover; a horseshoe (or another so-called "good luck" charm); two 5-cent plastic cars whose front ends you have heated over a flame until they have caved in, looking as if they had collided in an accident. Place a piece of string or yarn on a flannelboard (or any other wooden board or cardboard large enough) to form a large heart. Slant straight pins into the string every four or five inches, to hold it in place if necessary. Stick several pins in a group in the center of the heart, letting them protrude about a half inch, so that they can hold the cars.

TO BE safe is to be free from harm and danger. You'd think that *everybody* would try to live safely. But many people don't pay any attention to rules that have been passed to help them to keep alive and safe. Does it surprise you to know that in 1953, there were 38,300 people killed in auto accidents in the 48 states of the United States? And that 40 children are killed every day in auto accidents, in the United States alone ?

If you were to ask some people if they could do anything to avoid many of these accidents, they would shake their heads and say, "No, it's just fate. What is supposed to be is supposed to be. Some folks are supposed to die in accidents." Do you think they are right? No, for if many of those who were killed had known and obeyed the traffic laws, they might be alive today.

If you were to ask certain others what they do to avoid accidents and keep safe, they would say, "I carry a rabbit's foot, or a four-leaf clover, or some other 'good luck' charm, and I have a horseshoe hanging over my door [show these if you have them]. These things help to keep me from having accidents or any other bad luck." Do you think that a rabbit's foot. a four-leaf clover, or any other so-called good-luck charm can possibly keep you from accidents or death?

What are some of God's answers to those who believe in fate or in luck? Who controls the length of each life? Is it blind fate—what's supposed to be is supposed to be— or is it God who made us? King David gives us the answer in one of his psalms. David said to God in prayer, "My times are in thy hand" (Ps. 31:15a). David was going through times of great danger. Enemies were trying to kill him. But David fully trusted the Lord. David believed that the Lord was controlling his life. He believed that God knew all the dangers he was going through, God cared for him, God was keeping him safe even in hard places, and God absolutely controlled his "times," or the length of his life. Our times, too, are in *God's hands*. Fate has nothing to do with the length of our lives.

What about luck? Does God have anything to say about charms? Yes, God definitely warns us against them. He calls charmers and others who attract people with good-luck charms and fortunetelling "an abomination" to Him (Deut. 18:9-12). No, we cannot and must not depend on fate or any so-called "lucky" thing to keep us safe.

What will keep us safe as we walk or bicycle back and forth to school and Sunday School, crossing streets and dodging traffic? What will keep us safe as we ride in cars? Yes, knowing and obeying traffic laws! If the driver of a car pays no attention to speed limits, no-passing zones, stop signs, danger signs, and other important traffic laws, he is deliberately taking his life into his own hands— and other lives, too.

But as important as it is to keep our bodies safe, it's even more important to keep our hearts, or souls, safe [point to heart on board]. In the Bible, God has given us definite laws and warnings, stop signs, restricted speeds, no-passing zones, and other valuable and necessary information on how to avoid eternal death and keep safe in His sight. Will merely *knowing* the Ten Commandments and many New Testament Scriptures, even being able to repeat them from memory, keep you safe from eternal death? No, you must *obey* God's safety laws and His warnings.

Sometimes, when we ride in cars, we get provoked at traffic rules and think we could improve them. We forget that many traffic experts have worked for months and even years to work out the best rules for everyone. Also, as we live our Christian lives, God's rules may not suit us and we think we could improve *them.* But God's way is always the *right way,* the *best way,* and the *only way* for us to follow.

If we break some traffic laws, should we be angry at policemen whose duty it is to make us keep the law of our land? No, when they give us a ticket for disobeying some law, they are doing what they are paid to do.

How about our attitude toward our parents, Sunday School teachers, and pastor, who, much more lovingly than any traffic officer, try to keep us from breaking God's laws? Should we refuse and resist their warnings and help? Or should we wisely take their advice? One timely proverb from God's Word reminds us, "When the wise is instructed, he *receiveth* knowledge" (Prov. 21:11). Our parents and teachers instruct us, not to be mean to us, but to help us to keep away from dangerous and harmful places and companions, and to be *safe* both now and for all time in the life to come. We will be wise, if we receive their instruction in a humble spirit.

Did you know that many auto accidents start in people's hearts? [Point to heart again.] From records that have been compiled, it has been found that *selfishness* is a chief cause for accidents. People think only of themselves, their own plans, their own wants, their own way. They want everyone else to get out of their way. They zoom impatiently through yellow lights. They pass cars on hills and curves. They drink beer or even more in-toxicating liquor, even though they have been told that a single bottle of beer slows up their mental alertness and ability to act quickly in emergencies. They just do not think of others. And the results are accidents. [Place wrecked cars inside the heart.] Where did these accidents start? Yes, in their hearts.

The records also show that *anger* often causes accidents, for a driver filled with anger forgets about everything else. He forgets to be careful, and may be so angry that he doesn't care what happens. When a driver is in that condition, accidents are bound to happen.

Again, records show that when *worry* fills one's heart and mind, the result often is a terrible accident. Yes, many accidents start in the heart.

But salvation and spiritual blessings, too, begin in the heart (Rom. 10:10). When Jesus becomes our Saviour, He is able to keep our hearts in perfect peace (Rom. 5:1; Isa. 26:3). Because we trust the Lord and His Word, we feel completely safe in Him. The more we let Him control our hearts, the safer we feel. Our Lord is able to keep us from falling into sin (Jude 24) and to provide a way of escape for us when we are tempted to do wrong (I Cor. 10:13) IF we *want* Him to and continue to trust and obey Him. Let's sing the chorus of *Trust and Obey*, that hymn we know so well, changing the words of the third line:

> Trust and obey,
> For there's no other way
> *To be kept safe in Jesus,*
> But to trust and obey.

Light-of-the-World Christians

THEME Witnessing as a shining light for Christ.

MATERIALS A kerosene lamp; some sand and scraps of metal; enough kerosene to fill the lamp; matches.

HERE'S an old-fashioned kerosene lamp, to give an up-to-date lesson on what it really means to live or shine for Jesus [hold up lamp]. Many lamps that look like this are electrified today, but in your great-grandparents' time they filled such lamps with kerosene to light their homes at night so that they could read or sew.

Jesus told some followers who believed in Him, "Ye are the light of the world" (Matt. 5:14). But what did Jesus say about those who would not believe in Him? He said they preferred darkness to light because their deeds were evil (John 3:19).

We can think of this kerosene lamp as a believer in Christ who is now, or was in times past, a true light-bearer, one who brought God's light to those in the darkness of sin. Paul the Apostle, David Livingstone, Mary Slessor, and D. L. Moody were well known light-bearers for Jesus.

Did you ever hear of light-bearer Mary Slessor? Mary was a young Scotch woman who went as a missionary to Africa in 1876. To that land known as the "dark continent," a fierce, wild country of thick jungles, whose people's minds were darkened with weird superstitions, frail young Mary went with the light of Christ. Mary didn't live in a comfortable brick bungalow, but in a crude hut, with and like the natives. She ate their food, went barefoot, even ran through the jungle at night to help those in need, unafraid of poisonous snakes or wild animals, trusting God to keep her and to help her shine for Him.

What made Mary such a light for God? Was she trying to earn a lot of money, or to become popular? No! She shone because she constantly brought Christ, the Light of the world, to Africans whose hearts were filled with dark superstitions (John 8:12).

But there had been a time when Mary was of no more value to God than this pile of sand and scrap metal [show sand and some metal in bulk or sheet form]. But much like sand is made into glass, and metal is changed by those who know how, into lamps, so Mary Slessor and all of us who know Jesus as our Saviour are changed by Jesus, the Master-Changer, and made into lamps for Him.

This lamp is complete, having the part that holds the oil, the wick, the adjuster of the wick, and the flue or chimney [point to each as you mention it]. But it is not ready to shine. If you were to buy a kerosene lamp, this is all that you'd receive. But no matter how attractive or how well made your lamp would be, it would not shine, just as it is. If you'd light the wick [illustrate], it would burn very little, and would soon go out. Why?

The lamp needs to be filled with kerosene, the proper *fuel*. And if *you* are going to shine for Jesus, so that others will be attracted to the Saviour, as He has planned for you to shine (Matt. 5:16), you must be filled with the Holy Spirit (Eph. 5:18). Who is He? The Holy Spirit is the Partner of God the Father and Jesus Christ the Son. And He comes to live in the hearts of believers, to keep us thinking about Christ and to help make God's Word clear to us (John 14:16, 17, 26). As we grow in our Christian lives, through prayer and Bible study, the Holy Spirit can fill us more and more.

If this lamp were filled with *water*, you might think that it is kerosene, at first, because water *looks* like kerosene. But when darkness would come and you'd try to light the lamp, there would be no light—only a little sputtering when you'd light the wick. The same is true of us as lights of the world. Only as we let the Holy Spirit fill us with Himself can we shine as Jesus has told us to.

One dark midnight two men were letting their lights shine for Christ, as lamps that were filled and burning, even though they were in a damp prison and their backs were bleeding from severe beatings, and their feet were stuck through holes in a wooden plank, called stocks. Perhaps these men *outwardly* looked like some other prisoners. But *inwardly* they were different, for the Holy Spirit was filling their hearts with courage and love and praise to the Lord. Though their trials were heavy and the midnight hour was black, their Christ-like lights didn't sputter and go out. Instead, they shone brightly as these Christian prisoners sang praises to God (Acts 16:25-31).

Suddenly the Lord caused a terrible earthquake to rock the prison, and the doors flew open. The keeper was about to kill himself, because he was sure that the prisoners must have escaped. If they had, *he* would have been executed by the Roman government. But Paul, one of the singing prisoners, shouted at him, "Do yourself no harm, for we are all here!" The frightened jailer then called for a light. Not only was a lamp brought, but Paul and his companion Silas showed this needy, desperate man the "true Light," the Saviour Jesus Christ. Paul and Silas could lead this needy man to Christ because they themselves were filled and shining Christians.

An important part of this lamp is the wick, made of twisted cotton threads. This wick reaches down into the kerosene, or oil, and draws it upward. Can you see how this wick is somewhat like your talents, your personality? The wick itself cannot give light, but as it draws the oil up from the base of the lamp, the light shines [light lamp].

Like the wick, by yourself you can do nothing (John 15:5). But you can shine for the Lord through your talents of singing, speaking, playing, helping, or simply smiling, if you draw on the power of the Holy Spirit.

When you see a lamp burning, you don't notice the

wick—you notice the light. People who don't know the Lord Jesus should not see what a remarkable person *you* are, but should be able to see the Lord Jesus Himself shining through you.

Here's the lamp's adjuster, which makes the flame little or big. This adjuster is like your will. You can either yield your life to Jesus to shine [turn up wick], or try to get along with your own dim light [turn wick down].

Another vital part of the lamp is the glass flue, or chimney. Take it away and the light flickers [illustrate]. If the wind blows a little, the light goes out [show this by blowing out light]. So the flue's job is to protect the flame from drafts. The flue is not on the lamp to call attention to itself; it is there to help the lamp to shine brightly. Drafts of doubt may threaten to put out your light for the Lord, or at least make it flicker, but not if you have on the protecting flue of prayer.

The wick in this lamp will last for months. But every day that the lamp is used it has to be filled and the chimney must be cleaned, so that the light can keep shining brightly. We too must trust the Lord to fill us with His love and strength every day and be always clean by quickly confessing our sins to Him (I John 1:9). Simply because we used to shine for Christ is not enough. *We must keep on shining.*

Let's thank the Lord now for the picture He has placed in His Word of our shining as bright, clean, useful lights, so that we can effectively attract others to Him.

Processed and Powerful

THEME Good and evil uses of the tongue (including witnessing).

MATERIALS Small, rounded stick; small block of wood, slightly hollowed out; a piece of steel and a small hard rock; a box of wooden phosphorous matches; a box of safety matches or package of paper safety matches; a block of wood (a short 2″ x 4″ will do); a large candle.

THE Bible mentions two little things that, rightly used, can bring a great deal of comfort and happiness, or, if wrongly used, can cause much pain and sorrow. Would you like to guess what they are?

Turn to James 3:5 in your Bible. The first one who finds that verse may read it aloud. Yes, these two things are a *tongue* and a little *fire*. They are alike in that they both can bring either blessing or terrible destruction.

Men value fire because it gives them warmth and light and cooks their food. To get fire American Indians used to put the ends of sticks into hollowed-out dry blocks of wood which contained bits of dry leaves [illustrate]. Then they'd spin their sticks back and forth between the palms of their hands, faster and faster, until the friction caused heat which would ignite the leaves. By blowing and adding more fuel, they were able to build full-sized fires. Have you boys ever done this?

Even in the early 1880's, men still used crude methods to light fires. The great English author, Charles Dickens, complained that it took 30 minutes to start a fire with pieces of steel and flint (strike steel against the rock, making sparks).

But whether the man lighting his fire was a 19th-century Englishman with flint and steel, or an Indian using sticks, or a modern man with a match [hold up a match], the fire that was started could bring either good or harm. It could cook his food, and light and warm his home, or it could destroy his possessions and burn him. And God says that your tongue is like fire!

You may not have thought of it before, but your tongue can either bring warmth and blessing to other people, or it can scorch them. When your tongue speaks right words, it gives out friendliness, love, and generosity. The tongue of a Gospel preacher brings God's message to his congregation. The tongue of a singer thrills an audience. Many Christians use their tongues to explain the way of salvation to others. Yes, a tongue can—and should—be like a controlled fire—warming and enlightening.

But your tongue can also "burn" another person. Do you know how? What about cruel words that you speak angrily or thoughtlessly? Once a little blind girl was about to play in a circle game when one of the children blurted out, "You can't play with us—*you're blind!*" That brave little blind girl left the circle with her heart almost broken, because someone's tongue got out of control.

Again, tongues can tell lies and can speak proud words that cause hatred and even wars between countries. Then the tongue becomes, as the Bible says, like a raging fire that can't be stopped until tremendous damage has been done. It's sad but true that even Christians' tongues sometimes get out of control.

It's also true that some Christians burn brightly *for the Lord,* while other Christians don't show God's light and power. Let's let this piece of wood [a short 2" x 4"] represent a Christian who is satisfied that *he* knows the Lord, and doesn't care about helping others to become Christians. This block of wood, in its present form, isn't very useful, and it certainly doesn't have the power to shine for God. But men can process this block and make it into many, many matches. Made into matches, this piece could help provide light and warmth for many people.

Matchmaking is an interesting process. First, a piece of wood is cut into match-size sticks. These sticks are then inserted into a plate with round holes that holds each match firmly as it travels through the factory, right side up and upside down, dipping in one chemical solution after another, five times!

First, the anti-afterglow and *drying dip*, which fireproofs the matchstick against double-burnings.

Second, the *paraffin dip* to carry the flame easily from the match tip to the wood.

Third, the *base dip* in a solution that will burn, but which protects the matches against striking fire by rubbing together while in the box.

Fourth, the *tip dip*, which places the head on the base and allows striking of the flame by friction, or "scratching."

Fifth, a *hard coating dip*, which protects the head from moisture in the air.

All that treatment just for little matches? Yes, but remember that just *one* little match can do much more than this big block of wood. Is that because the match is made out of better wood? Or because it's stronger; or prettier? No—the match has been processed and has *power* given to it!

Do you want to be more than a useless "piece-of-wood" Christian? Yes, you want to be a Christian with power to shine for God. Jesus told His disciples, "Ye are the light of the world" (Matt. 5:14). Jesus meant that they were to live so that His own light, power, and warmth would shine out to others—after they had gone through His processing, testing, empowering period. Jesus' processing changed those comparatively useless men into shining lights for Himself.

And the Lord will process and prepare *you*, much more thoroughly than manufacturers prepare matches, if you believe Him and ask Him. God's directions in the

70

Bible are something like the strong plate that will hold and lead you through His preparation processes, so that you will become a bright witness for Him, anywhere, any time.

Some matches [hold up safety or paper matches] will strike only in certain places. They are something like Christians who can testify only in church or when they're with other Christians [strike a safety match on its own container]

But these "strike-anywhere" matches [hold up phosphorous matches] are like Christians who can shine anywhere for Christ.

In 1943, a man discovered how to treat matches so they would light even after being in water for eight hours! This is amazing, but it's not so wonderful as God's processing, which enables trusting Christians to witness for Christ even when Satan is using all his tricks to "snuff out" their light! (II Cor. 4:3, 4).

This match [show], though so small, can light a big candle [illustrate]. It can also light an oven, so that we can enjoy baked food, or a fire in a furnace, so that we can enjoy warm homes.

Think carefully. What kind of Christian are you? Are you just a "piece-of-wood" Christian, satisfied that you know the Lord as your own Saviour, but not caring about helping others to become Christians?

Or are you a Christian who sometimes lets his light shine for the Lord, but other times uses his light as a burning, damaging fire which hurts others?

Or are you the kind of Christian who goes every day to God's Word for directions, who talks often to the Lord in prayer, and allows God to process and control you, so that you have His power and let your light shine steadily for God, and your tongue bring blessings to others? All of you who want to be *that* kind of Christian sing with me, *Lord, keep me shining for Thee.*

Cracked-corn or Popcorn Christians

THEME Sharing Christian qualities amid trials and testings.

MATERIALS Unpopped popcorn, of different colors if possible. Try to get white, yellow, and black. Optional: a small bag of popped corn to give each child at end of the lesson.

H AVE you seen your mother use any of these things: ready-made biscuits, powdered milk, cake mix, frozen vegetables or fruits? What would your great-grandparents have thought if they could have seen people today taking biscuits out of a can, cake and milk out of a box, and fresh fruits and vegetables from a freezer? They probably would have thought that they had been carried off to a land of magic.

But do you know that there is one food we eat today, that the South American Indians used to eat even before Columbus discovered America? What am I holding in my hand? [Show popcorn.] The Inca Indians of Peru were raising and popping popcorn more than 500 years ago. Those Indians popped it with heat and enjoyed it as much as we do.

The Incas had all sorts of corn—not little, undeveloped corn fields, but corn that was highly developed. Some of their kernels of corn were as big as a quarter, and the colors ranged through red, pink, blue, black, and brown. But were the large, beautifully colored grains *popcorn*? No, for the grains of popcorn then, as well as now, were very small. Popcorn grows on small plants, and the ears are also small. It is neither the size nor beauty of the kernels that make popcorn different from regular corn, but, rather, its unusual inner quality.

Popcorn, like a true Christian, is different not on the *outside,* but on the *inside.* It is having Christ in one's heart that makes a person a Christian. Christians cannot boast of their *own* power, their *own* strength, their *own* wisdom—it is the unusual quality of Christ *in* them that makes them different.

The true character or nature of popcorn is not fully appreciated until it has been tested or heated by fire. It is then that the moisture inside the kernel turns to steam which builds up great pressure. Finally the outer skin bursts, and then the entire inside of the kernel puffs out. Grains of any other kind of corn may look the same, but they will not explode, as popcorn does. They only crack and parch, for they do not have the power to withstand heat. But popcorn has. The unusual quality of popcorn doesn't show up until fire is put to it.

To encourage believers in Christ, God's Word advises us, "Think it not strange concerning the fiery trial which is to try you" (I Pet. 4:12). All Christians should *expect* to go through fiery testings. For God allows these, to test our faith in Him. You remember that it was in a fiery furnace that Daniel's three young friends trusted God and were delivered from fierce flames (Dan. 3). It was in the fire of bitter persecution that the first martyr, Stephen, proved his faith in his Saviour by dying for Him (Acts 7:55, 56). The true character of Christians shows up when circumstances are hard. Then their inner strength is revealed.

It doesn't make any difference what color you are— it's how you react when you are tried. There are yellow, black, and white popcorn kernels [show these if you have them]. But after fire is put to them, they all turn white.

Popcorn tastes better when it is seasoned with salt. Did you know that God's Word tells us to have our conversation, our words and actions, "seasoned with salt"? (Col. 4:6). Perhaps this is because salt seasons, purifies, and preserves. Our life should be seasoned with the salt of God's Word, His kindness, and His love. But you say,

"Salt doesn't stick to popcorn very well without butter." So we heat butter till it's like oil and pour it over the popcorn, then season it with salt. My how good it tastes!

Oil is often linked to the Holy Spirit. As we give Him control, He will make God's Word, like "salt," season and purify us and make our testimony far more appealing.

People are more interested in the final product of popcorn than they are in the unpopped kernels. And they are far more interested in "seasoned" Christians whose lives show the unusual inner qualities of Christian love—joy, peace, longsuffering, gentleness, goodness, faith, meekness, and self-control (Gal. 5:22, 23). True Christians show these Christ-like qualities when they go through the heat of trials or testings. And their speech and actions are seasoned with God's wonderful grace.

Are you the kind of Christian who just dries up and cracks when troubles come? Or are you the popcorn kind of Christian who, when tested by fiery trials, snaps out of your hard kernel of self and comes out pure and white? Let's ask the Lord now to make each of us that kind of Christian.

Christian "Space Men"

THEME The second coming of Christ.

MATERIALS Boy's space hat (if possible); some plastic space men (these may be purchased at a dime store); any other articles connected with space travel. Announce this service a week in advance and let the children bring whatever items they have which are related to travel in outer space.

D O YOU boys and girls enjoy stories and pictures about men flying through outer space? Maybe you've pretended that you were space men and women, wearing futuristic-looking suits. But all the time you knew you were just playing.

Did you know that the United States government has laid plans for flights many miles above the earth, much higher than any planes fly now? The plans have advanced so far that a high-altitude suit has been developed and actual tests are underway in preparation for great space flights. All this might seem fantastic, hard to understand, hard to believe, but we believe it because the government has announced it and after all, it is no more difficult to believe in space flights than in robot planes which we know are actually flying through space without pilots to guide them.

Forty days after the Lord Jesus rose from the dead, He went back up to heaven. His stunned disciples were looking "steadfastly toward heaven as He went up," when two angels told them, "Ye men of Galilee, why stand ye gazing up into heaven? This same Jesus which is taken up from you into heaven, *shall so come in like manner* as ye have seen him go into heaven" (Acts 1:10, 11). To many folks, the fact that the Lord Jesus Christ will come again, descending from heaven into the clouds, to receive those who are ready to meet Him, is harder to believe than the story of men flying through space. Yet, much more than we believe reports from our government about space ships and high-altitude flying suits, though we cannot understand all the details, do we believe the record that God has given in His Word concerning the glorious appearing of our Lord and Saviour, Jesus Christ. (Read aloud I Thessalonians 4:16, 17.)

Though we cannot at all understand just how the Lord Jesus will appear in the air and all believers will be caught up to meet Him—first, all the Christians who have died and then all who are still alive—we know that God's Word and His promises are sure. Dan, will you read a verse which clinches our faith and trust in God's Word? It's Matthew 24:35. Now Wayne, you read verse 44 of this same chapter, please. What does this verse tell us to do? That's it—"Be . . . ready!" What for? For the coming of Jesus, who is here referred to as the Son of man.

Perhaps we shall better understand how we can be ready for Jesus' return to take all Christians to be with Him forever, if we consider some of the preparation that men must go through before they're ready to fly through space.

What qualifications must men have who are chosen for a space crew? They must pass all sorts of tests. They must be able to stand being encased in a suit of thick rubber with a heavy plastic helmet that looks like a fish bowl. After they put on the suit, they must be able to breathe the artificial air that is provided through various tubes. Their blood pressure is tested in a cylinder that produces much the same sensation as they will have on the actual flight. Their nerves, muscles, breathing, pulse and heartbeat, their courage, fear, weariness, boredom, perspiration—everything is checked.

The special suit, provided and paid for by the government, especially interests us. Scientists who have designed this suit have tried to take into consideration every known need of space men. You see, even in the upper part of the earth's lower atmosphere there is no air to breathe; and when one gets up to eight to twelve miles above sea level, his body fluids boil! So the special suit, costing thousands of dollars, has been made to stand up under many tests, in order to provide protection for the men who are chosen for the flight. In other words, space fliers must meet definite requirements before they can fly through space.

That, of course, recalls the specific requirements that we must meet if we expect to be caught up into the air to meet the Lord Jesus on His return. God's requirements, clearly described in His Word, the Bible, are that we:

1. Realize we're sinners, and can't get to heaven by ourselves (Rom. 3:23; Eph. 2:8, 9);
2. Believe that God's Son, Jesus, took our sins upon Him when He died on the cross (II Cor. 5:21; I Pet. 2:24);
3. Ask the Lord to save us from our sins (Rom. 10:13).

Only by meeting these requirements can we hope to meet the Lord Jesus in the air when He returns to claim all who belong to Him. Only those who are wearing God's garment of salvation will be ready to meet Jesus.

Did you know that the Bible compares our *salvation* to a *garment?* In Isaiah 61:10 we read, "I will greatly rejoice in the Lord, my soul shall be joyful in my God; for he hath clothed me with the garments of salvation, he hath covered me with the robe of righteousness." When we accept Jesus as our Saviour, it is as though the Lord put on us the protective garment of salvation. All of us who have on *that* garment, who have met His requirements, may confidently expect to meet the Lord in the air some day.

Since government officials have gone to so much trouble to provide for the safety of space explorers, do you think that they would grant a man the privilege of flying into outer space who would refuse to wear *that*

77

suit? Of course not! The suit is necessary; it is not only required but provided. Therefore a man would be foolish even to consider attempting a space flight without it. Let's pray together now that none of us will be so foolish as to be without the garment that our heavenly Father so generously provides, when the Lord Jesus comes back to take those who love Him to be with Him forever.